In the Beginning God
Created the Earth...

the Trees

The Bible Tells Me So Press

In the Beginning God Created the Earth...
the Trees

A children's book produced by
The Bible Tells Me So Press

PUBLISHED BY
THE BIBLE TELLS ME SO CORPORATION
WWW.THEBIBLETELLSMESO.COM

First Edition, November 2021

The wonderful, strong, and useful trees
could never have happened
by chance or accident.
They are far too
amazing
for that.

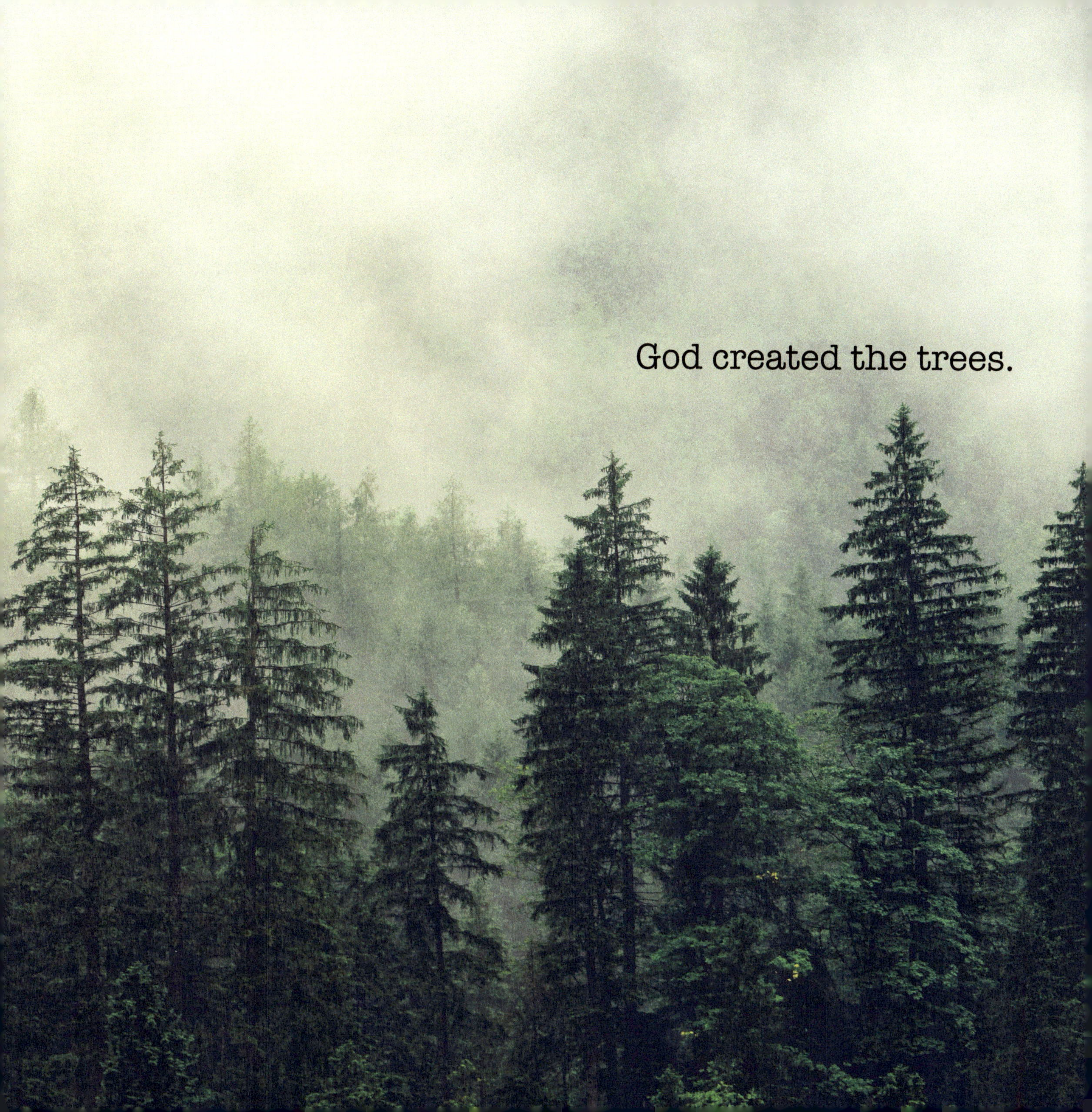

God created the trees.

There are about 60,000
different kinds of trees
on the earth.

Trees are
beautiful,
strong,
and
majestic
because
our God who
created them
is all of
those things
as well.

Some trees have leaves that change color in autumn right before they fall to the ground for winter.

Their blazingly
bright colors
are beautiful
and inspiring.

Other trees keep their leaves all year round.
Those trees are called
evergreen trees.

Some
evergreen
trees have
leaves that are long and
pointy, like narrow,
green
needles.

The tallest trees in the world
are the giant redwoods in California.
They can grow to be
over 310 feet tall.

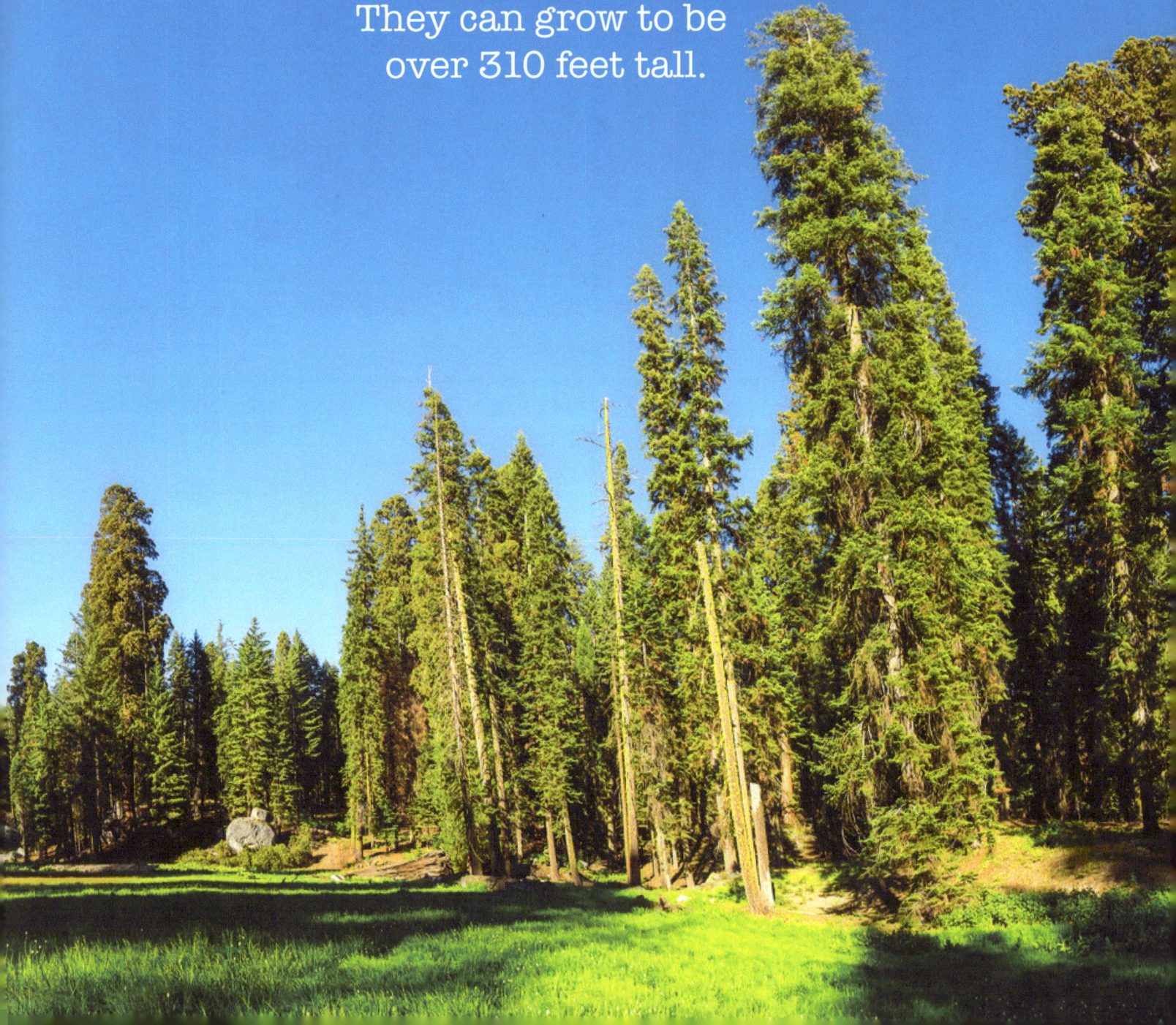

That's taller
than the
Statue
of Liberty!

Every
leaf is
an amazing
little factory.
Through a process
called photosynthesis,
plants mix water from the roots
with sunlight and carbon dioxide
to make food for themselves
and clean air
for us!

That's right!
Plants help to make
the fresh air
that we breathe.

Photosynthesis is just one of many incredible examples that show the wisdom of God, our great Creator.

But there's more

Some large trees lift over 100 gallons of water up through their root system every day.

That's
enough
to fill the
fuel tanks
of five cars every 24 hours!

Trees provide
warm and safe homes
for all kinds of animals,
such as squirrels
and birds.

Trees also provide warm and safe homes for us!

The strong wood
that we use to make
our homes
and our furniture
comes from trees.

And, did you know...

the wood from trees
contains cellulose and oils
that make it possible
for us to have things like
ping-pong paddles,
ping-pong balls,
toothpaste,

paper, pencils,
and even ice cream?

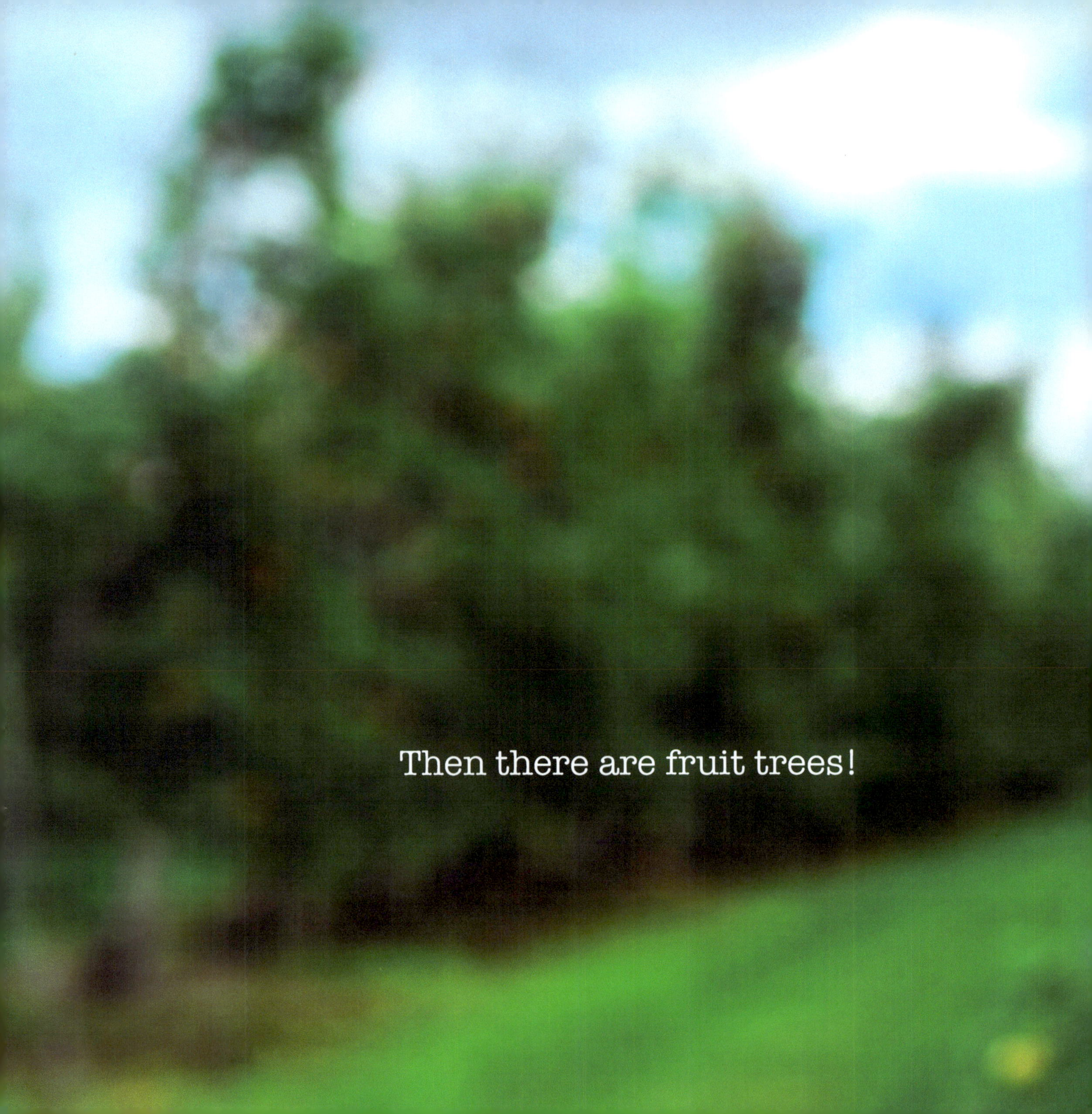

Then there are fruit trees!

There are many different kinds of fruit trees that bear many different kinds of fruit.

Have you ever considered an orange?

Each one is filled with little edible packets of delicious and healthy orange juice.

And the
whole thing
is wisely covered
in a biodegradable,
protective skin,
so we can carry it with us
and enjoy it
wherever we go.
Oranges are
amazing!

Bananas
are too!

And
so are all
the other kinds
of fruit that come
from trees
(like these
peaches).

So, the next time
you use a
chair,

write
on
some
paper,

or even enjoy
some fresh, clean air,
take a moment to
thank the Lord
for creating...

the trees.

And out of the ground
Jehovah God caused to grow
every tree that is pleasant to the sight
and good for food.

Genesis 2:9a

For more
books, videos, songs, and crafts,
visit us online at
TheBibleTellsMeSo.com

The Bible Tells Me So.com ™

Standing on the Bible and growing!

www.ingramcontent.com/pod-product-compliance
Lightning Source LLC
Chambersburg PA
CBHW042116040426
42449CB00002B/55

9 781948 940252